THE THRIVING PARENT

PRACTICAL GUIDE TO RAISING YOUR BOY TEEN WITH ADHD

TAYLOR WELLNESS

Disclaimer:

The information provided in this book is intended to be general in nature and is not a substitute for professional advice. The author and publisher assume no responsibility for any errors or omissions and disclaim any liability, loss, or risk that may be incurred as a consequence of the use and application of any of the contents of this book.

TABLE OF CONTENT

ADHD

INTRODUCTION

Welcome to "The Thriving Parent," a heartfelt guide designed to navigate the intricate journey of parenting a teenage boy with ADHD. As a parent, you've embarked on a unique adventure, one that presents both challenges and extraordinary opportunities for growth.

Understanding ADHD: A Brief Overview

Before we delve into the practical aspects of parenting, let's take a moment to understand ADHD and its impact on your child's life. Attention Deficit Hyperactivity Disorder is more than a collection of symptoms; it's a distinctive way of experiencing the world. Acknowledging this is the first step toward creating a supportive and thriving environment for your teen.

In these pages, we'll explore not only the nuances of ADHD but also the emotional landscape of parenting a child with this condition. From the initial realization that your son has ADHD to the empowering strategies that will guide him toward a fulfilling future, this guide is your companion through every step of the journey.

A Shared Experience

Parenting a teenager with ADHD can be isolating, but you are not alone. This book is written not just as a guide but as a companion from someone who understands the challenges and joys you face. Drawing from both professional insights and personal experiences, this guide aims to bridge the gap between knowledge and action.

Setting the Stage for Thriving

As we embark on this journey together, let's embrace the uniqueness of your parenting experience. It's not just about managing symptoms; it's about unlocking the potential within your child. In the chapters that follow, we'll navigate through the stages of childhood and adolescence, providing you with practical tools and empowering insights to foster resilience, build strong connections, and ensure your son not only copes with ADHD but thrives.

Get ready to embark on a path of understanding, growth, and, most importantly, thriving. Your role as a parent is pivotal, and by the end of this guide, you'll be equipped with a dynamic action plan to guide your son toward a future filled with possibilities.

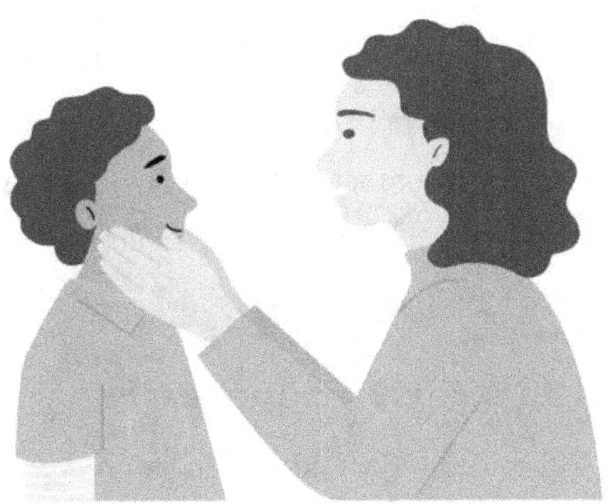

CHAPTER 1: COMING TO TERMS: MY SON HAS ADHD. NOW WHAT?

Welcome to the beginning of your journey, a journey that begins with acknowledgment and understanding. In this chapter, we'll navigate the initial waves of realization and emotion that often accompany the discovery that your son has ADHD. It's a crucial starting point, laying the foundation for the thriving parent you are destined to become.

Recognizing the Signs

As a parent, the realization that your son may have ADHD can be a mix of emotions - confusion, concern, and perhaps even a sense of relief that there's finally an explanation for certain behaviors. To begin, let's explore the signs and symptoms, unraveling the mystery that is ADHD.

Exercise: Reflective Journaling

Take a moment to reflect on your own observations. What behaviors or patterns have you noticed in your son that led you to consider the possibility of ADHD? Journaling these thoughts can be a powerful way to gain clarity and set the stage for the chapters ahead.

NOTES

Navigating Emotions as a Parent

Understanding and accepting the diagnosis is the first step, but it's not always an easy one. Parents often experience a range of emotions, from guilt and self-blame to anxiety about the future. It's essential to recognize and navigate these emotions constructively.

Practical Tip: Establish a Support System

Building a support system is crucial during this stage. Connect with other parents who have walked a similar path, seek guidance from professionals, and don't hesitate to lean on friends and family. Recall, you don't have to navigate this journey alone.

Empowering Mindset Shifts

As you come to terms with your son's ADHD, consider reframing your perspective. Instead of viewing ADHD as a limitation, see it as a unique way of thinking and experiencing the world. Embrace the strengths that often accompany ADHD, such as creativity, hyperfocus, and boundless energy.

Exercise: Strengths-Based Affirmations

List three positive qualities or strengths you've observed in your son. Use these as affirmations, reinforcing the unique and valuable aspects of his personality.

NOTES

Chapter 1 is not just about recognizing ADHD; it's about embracing the journey that lies ahead. As you navigate through the practical exercises and tips in this chapter, remember that you are laying the groundwork for a thriving parent-child relationship. The adventure has just begun, and by understanding and accepting, you're already on the path to becoming the thriving parent your son needs.

CHAPTER 2: TREATMENT OPTIONS FOR ADHD

As we embark on the journey of understanding and supporting your teen with ADHD, Chapter 2 is a crucial exploration of the various treatment options available. Beyond mere recognition, it's about taking proactive steps to empower both you and your son.

Treatment Modalities

ADHD is not a one-size-fits-all condition, and neither should the treatment approach be. In this chapter, we'll explore the diverse range of modalities available, from conventional medical interventions to holistic and lifestyle-based approaches.

Exercise: Personal Reflection

Before delving into the details, take a moment to reflect on your own preferences and beliefs about treatment. What aspects of conventional or alternative approaches resonate with you? Understanding your own mindset will guide your decisions as you explore the options.

NOTES

Medication and Its Considerations

Medication is often a topic laden with questions and concerns. We'll provide a comprehensive overview, addressing common misconceptions, potential benefits, and key considerations when deciding whether medication is the right path for your teen.

Practical Tip: Open Communication with Healthcare Providers

Establishing open and honest communication with healthcare providers is crucial. Make a list of questions and concerns, and don't hesitate to ask for clarification on any aspect of medication prescribed for your teen. Your active involvement is key to effective treatment.

Behavioral Therapies

Beyond medication, behavioral therapies offer valuable tools for managing ADHD symptoms. From cognitive-behavioral strategies to social skills training, this section will provide insights into practical approaches you can incorporate into your daily routine.

Exercise: Behavioral Strategy Journal

Create a journal to track behavioral strategies you've tried with your teen. Note the impact on specific situations and behaviors. This journal will serve as a valuable reference point as you refine and tailor your approach.

NOTES

Lifestyle Changes and Their Impact

Healthy lifestyle choices play a significant role in managing ADHD symptoms. From nutrition to sleep patterns, we'll explore how simple adjustments can have a profound impact on your teen's overall well-being.

Practical Tip: Establishing Routine

One of the most powerful lifestyle changes is the establishment of a consistent routine. Work with your teen to create a daily schedule that accommodates their unique needs and helps minimize the impact of ADHD symptoms.

Chapter 2 is not just about understanding treatment options; it's about taking the first steps toward an empowered and informed parenting approach. By exploring these diverse strategies and engaging in practical exercises, you're actively shaping a roadmap for your teen's thriving journey.

DISTRACTED

CHAPTER 3: INFANCY AND PRESCHOOL

The journey of raising a child with ADHD is a dynamic adventure that begins long before the teenage years. Chapter 3 delves into the formative stages of Infancy and Preschool, where the foundations for resilience and thriving are laid.

Early Signs and Observations

In the early years, recognizing potential signs of ADHD requires a keen eye and an understanding heart. This section explores the subtleties and nuances that may be indicative of ADHD in infancy and preschool.

Exercise: Developmental Milestones Reflection

Reflect on your child's developmental milestones. What moments stand out to you as unique or challenging? This exercise helps identify patterns and potential signs that may warrant further exploration.

NOTES

Parenting Strategies for the Early Years

Effective parenting strategies during infancy and preschool lay the groundwork for a resilient future. We'll explore practical approaches that nurture your child's strengths while addressing challenges head-on.

Practical Tip: Establishing Predictable Routines

Young children thrive on routine. Create a predictable daily schedule, incorporating consistent meal times, naps, and play. This not only provides stability for your child but also helps manage ADHD-related impulsivity.

Exploring Play as a Learning Tool

Play is a powerful tool for learning and development. Discover how specific types of play can engage your child's mind and promote cognitive and emotional growth.

Exercise: Mindful Playtime

Engage in a mindful playtime session with your child. Choose a simple activity, such as building blocks or drawing, and observe how your child responds. Notice any signs of focus or challenges and use this insight to tailor future play experiences.

Encouraging Positive Social Interactions

Early social interactions set the stage for future relationships. Learn how to foster positive connections with peers and family members, providing your child with a supportive social environment.

Practical Tip: Playdate Success Guide

Plan playdates with care, considering your child's energy levels and preferences. Provide structured activities and maintain open communication with other parents to ensure positive social experiences.

Chapter 3 is not just about navigating the early years; it's about embracing the joys and challenges of parenting a child with ADHD. By applying the insights gained from this chapter and actively participating in the exercises, you're cultivating a foundation that will support your child's journey toward thriving.

CHAPTER 4: THE ELEMENTARY YEARS

The journey continues as we step into the Elementary Years, a pivotal stage in your child's development. In this chapter, we'll navigate the unique challenges and opportunities that arise during these formative years, providing you with tools to foster not just academic success, but overall well-being.

School Challenges and Solutions

The academic landscape can pose distinct challenges for children with ADHD. We'll explore common hurdles and provide practical solutions to ensure a positive and successful experience within the school environment.

Exercise: Academic Strengths Assessment

Identify your child's academic strengths and preferences. This exercise involves observing your child's approach to various subjects and learning environments. Understanding these strengths will guide your collaboration with teachers and support personnel.

Building a Supportive Learning Environment

Create a home environment that complements your child's learning needs. From designated study spaces to effective time management strategies, discover ways to establish a supportive atmosphere that fosters focus and productivity.

Practical Tip: Homework Harmony

Homework time can be a source of stress. Develop a Homework Harmony plan, incorporating short breaks and clear expectations. This not only enhances productivity but also cultivates a positive attitude toward learning.

Nurturing Creativity and Passion

Children with ADHD often possess remarkable creativity and passion. Explore ways to channel these strengths into hobbies and extracurricular activities, fostering a sense of accomplishment and building self-esteem.

Exercise: Passion Exploration

Engage in a passion exploration activity with your child. Discover their interests and talents, and discuss how these passions can be integrated into their daily routine. This exercise promotes self-awareness and a sense of purpose.

NOTES

Fostering Positive Peer Relationships

Elementary school is a time of social development. Learn how to encourage positive peer relationships, providing your child with the social skills needed for healthy interactions.

Practical Tip: Social Skills Playbook

Create a "Social Skills Playbook" with your child, outlining scenarios and appropriate responses. Role-play these situations to build confidence and enhance social adaptability.

Chapter 4 is a stepping stone toward your child's flourishing journey. By understanding the challenges and implementing the exercises and tips provided, you're actively shaping an environment where your child can not only succeed academically but also thrive emotionally and socially.

CHAPTER 5: THE TEENAGE YEARS

The Teenage Years—a phase of self-discovery, independence, and, for parents, a dynamic shift in parenting strategies. This chapter delves into the intricacies of navigating adolescence with a teenager who has ADHD. It's a journey that demands flexibility, understanding, and a commitment to nurturing your teen's unique strengths.

Adolescent Development and ADHD

The intersection of ADHD and adolescence can bring forth both triumphs and trials. Explore the unique developmental aspects of adolescence, understanding how ADHD may manifest differently during this transformative period.

Exercise: Teenage Traits Reflection

Reflect on your teen's unique traits and characteristics. How do these align with typical teenage behavior, and what aspects may be influenced by ADHD? This exercise fosters a deeper understanding of your teen's individuality.

Communication Strategies for Teens

Effective communication becomes paramount during the teenage years. Learn strategies to foster open and constructive communication, allowing you to navigate challenges together and strengthen your parent-teen bond.

NOTES

Practical Tip: The Power of Active Listening

Practice active listening by summarizing your teen's thoughts and feelings during conversations. This simple yet powerful technique demonstrates empathy and encourages your teen to express themselves openly.

Balancing Independence and Structure

Teens crave independence, but structure remains essential. Discover how to strike a balance between granting autonomy and providing the necessary structure to support your teen's academic and personal growth.

Exercise: Co-Creation of Rules and Boundaries

Engage your teen in the co-creation of household rules and boundaries. This collaborative approach encourages a sense of ownership and responsibility, fostering a positive environment for growth.

Managing Academic Challenges

As academic demands intensify, teens with ADHD may face additional hurdles. Explore effective strategies for managing homework, exams, and other academic challenges, promoting a sense of accomplishment and self-efficacy.

Practical Tip: Time Management Toolbox

Develop a "Time Management Toolbox" with your teen, incorporating tools such as planners, apps, and visual schedules. This toolbox empowers your teen to take charge of their time and tasks.

Chapter 5 marks a pivotal juncture in your journey as a thriving parent. By understanding the unique challenges of the teenage years and actively participating in the exercises and tips provided, you're not just guiding your teen through adolescence but actively supporting their path toward resilience and well-being.

CHAPTER 6: WHEN MORE SUPPORT IS NEEDED

In the intricate dance of parenting a teenager with ADHD, there may come moments when additional support becomes essential. Chapter 6 is a guide through those pivotal times, offering insights into recognizing when extra help is needed and providing a roadmap for navigating support networks.

Collaborating with Schools and Professionals

Schools and professionals play key roles in your teen's development. Explore effective strategies for collaborating with educators, counselors, and other professionals to ensure your teen receives the support they need both academically and emotionally.

Exercise: School Support Checklist

Create a checklist of potential school support options. This exercise helps you identify specific areas where your teen may benefit from additional assistance, providing a foundation for discussions with school staff.

Exploring Support Networks

Building a strong support network is crucial for both you and your teen. Discover the importance of connecting with other parents, support groups, and community resources, creating a robust foundation for shared experiences and guidance.

Practical Tip: Establishing a Parent Support Circle

Initiate a parent support circle where you can share experiences, insights, and tips with other parents facing similar challenges. This network provides emotional support and a valuable exchange of practical strategies.

Understanding Therapeutic Interventions

Therapeutic interventions can offer valuable tools for managing ADHD-related challenges. Gain insights into various therapeutic approaches and how they can complement your parenting efforts.

Exercise: Personalized Therapy Goals

Work with your teen to identify personalized therapy goals. This exercise empowers your teen to take an active role in their therapeutic journey and ensures alignment with their unique needs and aspirations.

NOTES

Integrating Holistic Approaches

Holistic approaches encompass physical, mental, and emotional well-being. Explore how dietary adjustments, mindfulness practices, and other holistic strategies can contribute to your teen's overall thriving.

Practical Tip: Mindful Moments Ritual

Incorporate mindful moments into your daily routine. This could be a brief meditation, a nature walk, or shared quiet time. These rituals contribute to emotional balance and strengthen the parent-teen connection.

Chapter 6 is a guide through the landscapes of additional support, a resource for parents navigating the complex terrain of ADHD in adolescence. By actively participating in the exercises and tips provided, you're not just seeking support; you're creating a foundation for your teen's continued growth and resilience.

CHAPTER 7: PULLING IT ALL TOGETHER: THE DYNAMIC ACTION PLAN

Welcome to the culmination of your journey as a thriving parent. Chapter 7 is a roadmap, a dynamic action plan that weaves together the insights, strategies, and experiences gathered throughout this guide. It's time to synthesize your knowledge into a personalized approach that propels your teen toward not just surviving but truly thriving.

Creating a Tailored Parenting Strategy

Your teen is unique, and so should be your parenting approach. Discover how to synthesize the information gathered in previous chapters into a tailored strategy that addresses your teen's specific strengths, challenges, and aspirations.

Exercise: Strengths and Challenges Reflection

Reflect on your teen's unique strengths and challenges. Jot down specific examples and consider how these can be incorporated into your dynamic action plan. This exercise serves as the foundation for your personalized strategy.

<table>
<tr><td>NOTES</td></tr>
</table>

Building Resilience in Your Teen

Resilience is the cornerstone of thriving. Explore practical ways to instil resilience in your teen, fostering a mindset that not only overcomes challenges but grows stronger through them.

Practical Tip: The Resilience Toolbox

Create a "Resilience Toolbox" with your teen. This toolbox may include inspirational quotes, personal achievements, and coping strategies. Having a tangible resource reinforces the concept of resilience as a practical, accessible skill.

Fostering a Positive Parent-Child Relationship

The bond between parent and teen is a powerful force. Learn how to strengthen this connection through effective communication, empathy, and shared experiences, creating a foundation for mutual understanding and trust.

Exercise: Shared Goals and Dreams

Engage in a conversation with your teen about shared goals and dreams. This exercise not only deepens your connection but also aligns your dynamic action plan with your teen's aspirations, creating a joint venture toward success.

Adapting and Evolving with Your Teen

As your teen grows and evolves, so should your parenting strategy. Explore the art of adaptability, understanding when adjustments are needed and how to implement them effectively.

Practical Tip: Regular Check-Ins

Incorporate regular check-ins into your routine. These discussions provide a space for both you and your teen to share thoughts, concerns, and updates. It's an essential practice for maintaining open communication.

Chapter 7 marks the transition from information to action. By actively engaging in the exercises and tips provided, you're not just reading about parenting strategies—you're crafting a dynamic action plan that reflects your commitment to your teen's thriving journey.

CONCLUSION: EMBRACING THE JOURNEY - FROM AWARENESS TO THRIVING

As we reach the conclusion of this guide, take a moment to reflect on the transformative journey you've embarked upon. From the initial awareness that your son has ADHD to the creation of a dynamic action plan, you've embraced the challenges and celebrated the triumphs. The path to thriving parenting is ongoing, and it's one marked by resilience, understanding, and, most importantly, love.

Celebrating Progress and Achievements

Before we move forward, let's celebrate the progress made and the achievements, both big and small. Acknowledge the positive changes you've witnessed in your teen, and recognize the growth within yourself as a parent navigating the complexities of ADHD.

Exercise: Reflection and Gratitude Journal

Start a reflection and gratitude journal. Note down moments of progress, insights gained, and instances of resilience. This practice not only reinforces the positive aspects of your journey but also serves as a source of inspiration during challenging times.

NOTES

The Ever-Changing Landscape of Parenting

Parenting is an ever-evolving journey. As your teen grows and faces new experiences, your role as a parent adapts. Understand the beauty of this transformation and approach it with a mindset of continuous learning and adaptation.

Practical Tip: Mindfulness Moments with Your Teen

Incorporate mindfulness moments into your routine with your teen. Whether it's a shared walk, a creative activity, or a simple conversation, these moments foster connection and enhance the parent-teen relationship.

Expressing Love and Support

Your love and support are foundational pillars in your teen's life. Expressing this love goes beyond words—it's about creating an environment where your teen feels seen, heard, and accepted.

Exercise: Affirmation Jar

Start an affirmation jar for your teen. Write down affirmations that highlight their strengths, accomplishments, and unique qualities. Encourage your teen to contribute their own affirmations. This jar becomes a reservoir of positivity during challenging moments.

NOTES

Looking Forward with Hope and Optimism

As you look forward, do so with hope and optimism. Your teen's journey is a narrative of growth, and your role as a thriving parent is a testament to your commitment to their well-being.

Practical Tip: Goal-Setting Ritual

Engage in a goal-setting ritual with your teen. Establish short-term and long-term goals together, incorporating elements from your dynamic action plan. This ritual fosters a sense of purpose and shared commitment.

www.ingramcontent.com/pod-product-compliance
Lightning Source LLC
Chambersburg PA
CBHW071011260726
48661CB00007B/2903